Contents

I0491831

Introduction

Personal branding has never been more critical than it is today. With the advent and increasing popularization of social, digital media, there are, to put it mildly, so many brands out there. It has never been easier to create a platform and gain a successful following, but there has never been more competition. As a result of all this, branding has never been more essential.

The world is continually evolving, and keeping up with the trends is the only way to stay relevant, and having a quality personal brand is the best way to add value to a business.

Personal branding is for everyone, including women, regardless of the business type or industry. When you think about some of the biggest and most successful brands today, you also think about the people behind them. Naturally, the feelings and impressions you obtain about those entrepreneurs influence your perception of their work. No one is immune or exempt from the effects of branding, which is why you need to be ahead of the game, in control of your branding, and how the world perceives it.

There has never been a more immense amount of clutter for brands and businesses to be lost in.

No longer are we anonymous. We are all online. Having a personal brand is a way of controlling the narrative about who you are and what you stand for. It is a way of removing the barrier between you, your content creator, and your audience. It is the way you present yourself to your audience and how they will interact with you.

In marketing, they always talk about "noise." Having a clear, concise brand is the best way to cut through all that noise and be heard.

This eBook is for every woman who has an entrepreneurial dream and wants to be successful and recognized as an expert in the market. This book walks you through all the necessary steps to consider either before you begin to define your brand or to help you refine it to make it work better for you. This eBook will be split into several sections. The first section clearly defines what personal branding is and provides the key information needed to begin a personal brand. The second section builds upon the brand's concept that you have created and discusses appropriate media and content types. It highlights unique ways you can add authority and credibility to your brand.

This book begins by outlining exactly what personal branding is and why it is so essential. It then provides a step-by-step breakdown of the elements vital to shaping the foundation of your branding. Once the foundation has been laid, we will discuss the three keys to success: audience, authenticity, and credibility.

Following that, this eBook will describe some of the most popular media types for growing audiences and how you can harness them effectively. It will also summarize some of the best methods for content creation and growing your audience effectively. The next chapter will discuss the importance of analytics, which may not sound particularly interesting(!), but is quintessential to monitoring your outreach and engagement so that you can ensure the continued success of your content.

While, of course, most of the world is "online" now, it is also vital for your personal branding to extend into the rest of your life, so we will discuss some tactics for incorporating your brand into your everyday life.

This eBook will conclude by drawing on examples of successful brands and the associations they have with them. By analyzing prominent brands in your industry, you can emulate successful elements and improve their weaknesses when creating your brand.

This eBook will give you all the tools you need to create a personal branding strategy that is effective, credible, and successful. By implementing the information you will find in the following pages, you give your personal brand the best start possible.

A holistic approach to personal branding is described here. There is no one-size-fits-all method; there are only keys to success. You should adapt and alter these methods to make it appropriate for you and your goals. If you believe and trust the process, this eBook will give you the strongest possible foundation for your personal branding and future success.

The "What and Why" of Personal Branding

To firstly put it very, very simply, in essence, personal branding is the combination of who you are, what you are doing, and how you are doing it. It is your Purpose and your character; and how your audience perceives you.

But what does that mean?

The personalization of business is a key characteristic of how industries have changed in the last decade. Brands and marketing have become so incorporated and entangled within our daily lives that we are exposed to so many messages all day, often without noticing. Whereas in the past, the idea of a "brand" was exclusive to the business world. This is now an outdated concept.

These days, we are all brands, in effect. Even our personal social media account shares our brand with our friends and families—even if we do not always realize so. Our accounts are full of the things we care about, our interests, and the experiences we have. There are, often, a "highlight reel" of our lives, and they are all the things we want people to see us as.

Hence, personal branding.

Your personal brand is, in part, the relationship that your audience will have with you and your endeavor. It is what you want to be known for and how people will recognize you.

See the similarities? You likely already have a personal brand, of sorts. But, since you are probably already online, you may be wondering why you need to curate such a defined brand.

There is an abundance of reasons why having a strong personal brand is a requirement of a business.

Good personal branding helps attract more clients — it encourages engagement and feeds credibility. Rather than just being a mystery behind a screen, it shows that you are a real person, and therefore you have a higher level of influence over your audience.

In terms of a social media presence, people are often more inclined to follow another person than a random, faceless business account. Thus, good personal branding can encourage people to follow you as a person (a brand), and you will then introduce them to your business endeavors. This does not mean you have to have two accounts; you can be your business; it just means that your personality must shine through. Also, quality personal branding permits premium pricing.

Consumers pay more for a product that is backed by a quality and reputable brand. Just think about smartphones — despite numerous, cheaper options being readily available on the market, people tend to gravitate towards the same, more expensive brands. Without branding, you are just a product that is subject to intense competition; branding is what sets you and your price range apart. Consumers do not want to engage in business with a brand; instead, they would much rather interact with a person and know that, by proxy, they are helping another person live their dreams.

Therefore, good personal branding builds relationships with your audience — your interactions can be more authentic and unique. In contrast, your audience is more loyal, more engaged, and less likely to switch to a competitor's product.

It is how you differentiate yourself from everyone else and show that you are better, more qualified, and more credible than the rest. It increases your influence and persuasive power over your audience and is a fantastic way to add value to your endeavors.

Suppose you do not put in the time to develop your personal branding at the beginning of your venture. In that case, you will likely spend significantly more time later on undoing the damage of uncontrolled or chaotic branding. It is far better for you, professionally, developing a personal branding strategy, implementing it, and then adjusting and monitoring as your brand grows. This helps you remain up to date and, over time, will change organically.

It is far better to have a cultivated personal branding strategy from the outset than have to do damage control and completely reinvent your online presence.

Additionally, personal branding can be a pre-emptive form of marketing — it means you already have a good reputation in your audience's eyes. In the unfortunate circumstances that a bitter and disgruntled customer or unprofessional competitor tries to discredit you or spread negative misinformation, you will already have a robust platform. Already having a strong positive brand association makes your personal branding more stable and able to withstand shocks and will also provide less of a need for crisis management.

A strong personal brand creates a bond with your customers before you attempt to market your products or services to them. It means they are already on your team and want you to succeed.

Now that the idea of personal branding has been well-established in your mind, it is time to begin or revamp your own.

When reading the following chapters, you may find it helpful to stop and write down any thoughts you have or any answers to the questions posed. Understanding what and why and how things apply to your personal circumstances is essential in creating a valuable and credible unique branding strategy.

Creating your Personal Branding Strategy

To create a personal branding strategy that will be successful and add value to your venture, you first need to begin with a solid foundation. Much like with a house, if there are cracks in the foundation, it will not be long before the whole thing crumbles.

While setting out and clearly defining your personal brand may feel like it takes a lot of time to do — it is an upfront time investment. Once everything is visibly developed and strategized, it will make the remainder of the business planning a breeze.

However, it is also important to note that you should also be monitoring your branding strategy as your business unfolds. Monitoring should be a part of your admin — over time, it will become second nature. There will be more on this later, but first, let us utilize three questions to determine your brand's baseline.

As we go on, it is essential to remember that everything needs to be very clearly defined — if you are confused about your branding, your audience will be, too.

Just Before Your Brand Message

Before you begin laying the groundwork for your brand message, you'll want to make sure you thoroughly understand your market. This includes knowing who your potential customers are and who the competition is.

Here are a few ways to do this:

Research social media accounts from within your target audience. Pay close attention to what they tweet, how they respond to posts, what they like, and are most receptive to.

You'll want to do the same for your competitors. Focus on what kinds of content are posted that boosts engagement and how they've positioned themselves in the market.

Google your niche and analyze the top search results. Spend time on their websites, read their sales copy, and, if possible, purchase a few of their products so you can evaluate the type of content being offered.

Spend time within Facebook and subreddits, where people in your niche congregate to discuss common topics. Look for commonly asked questions and always lookout for ongoing discussions as it signifies a growing demand for help in specific segments of your market.

As you research, take as many notes as possible!

Look for who your average customer is and who your top competitors are. These are existing brands that have established themselves in your market. You can learn a lot from how they've positioned themselves as influential leaders and created a brand around that image.

It's essential that you truly understand your target audience before you create your brand. You want to build your brand image around what your average customer feels is most important to them. If you do this, you can't go wrong.

Once you've done your research, it's time to figure out your positioning statement. There are simply a few lines that describe your brand and solidifies your place in your market.

This isn't necessarily something you include on your website or business cards. It's merely an expression of how your products and services fill a specific need in your market. It gives people a compelling reason to buy from you.

The easiest way to develop a factual positioning statement or USP is to think of your brand as a customer.

- What would she/he be most interested in?
- What words would matter most?
- What offers or promises are expected?
- What questions do they have?

Thinking about your brand from a customer's perspective will help you choose a voice for your business that speaks to your audience and ultimately sets the tone for everything from marketing campaigns and social media updates to your website's content.

Defining Your Brand Message

When it comes to maximizing your income and establishing a strong foothold within your market, you absolutely need to build a unique and recognized brand that aligns with a clear and direct brand message.

Your brand message explains to potential customers what you have to offer and how committed you are to providing quality and value.

But here's the thing: you aren't the one who defines your brand message – your customers do!

It's your job to lay the groundwork as to what you want people to know about your business and then work towards supporting that identity through demonstrating knowledge, skills, and capabilities to deliver what was promised. However, your customers will be the ones who decide what your overall brand image is based on through their interactions with your business.

A well-defined strategic brand message can build instant credibility in your niche while helping you gain authority in your market and shape how customers perceive your business. It's quite often the critical difference between a well-structured online presence and a faltering business struggling to connect with its audience.

So, how can you build a recognized brand that provides a clear message that resonates with your market? Here is how you can go about it.

What is your Purpose?

This is a very abstract and confronting question. It is prudent to note that this phase of developing your personal branding strategy will require some deep reflection and reflective thinking. While it is intense, you will know yourself and what you want your dream life to look like better by the end.

You need to understand yourself, including your motivations and personality, to harness the best elements to shine in your personal branding.

Numerous things need to be considered, and different people value them in different ways. You need to decide which are the most important and most relevant attributes to be manipulated into your personal branding. It can be helpful to make a list of the following.

What are your:

- Past successes?
- Strengths?
- Goals?
- Experiences?
- Passions?
- Personality traits?
- Values?
- Beliefs?
- Interests?

What are the words that you want to be used in and associated with your brand? Write down as many things as you can think of for each of the categories mentioned above.

Then go through and highlight the ones that stand out to you. They should be the most important and most usable ones that can inspire your branding.

Do not be afraid to use your life! Your experiences, strengths, and ambitions are what make you, you. They are what will make your audience connect with you.

Who is your Audience?

Now that you have figured out a little more about who you are, you need to select your target audience. Defining your target audience means that you can tailor your content and marketing specifically and efficiently towards them.

Start by thinking about your target audience and what is most important to them. Once you've evaluated your niche, you will be able to position yourself so that you are directly addressing their most burning questions, concerns, and needs.

You need to gather as much intel on your market as possible, which you can do easily just by looking at the competition.

To do this, it can be helpful to come up with a particular image of a consumer.

First, what is the primary demographic of your target audience? This includes things like

- Age
- Location
- Gender
- Lifestyle
- Education
- Financial situation
- Technological use
- Family/living situation

Then, you need to think about them more psychologically.

- What do they want?
- What do they need?
- What challenges do they face?
- What do they believe in?
- What are their attitudes and behaviors?

What are other business owners and product developers offering your audience? What kind of products and services are they successfully selling?

Take things to social media and begin by evaluating social signals – which are clear indicators of current demand, popular, and selling well. The higher level of interaction, the more advertising dollars spent, and the more engagement, the better.

Defining your target audience as precisely as possible is a great way to ensure that your branding can be optimized to your potential future customers.

You need to make sure that the words you have chosen for your branding will also resonate and reflect well on your audience—otherwise, it leads to mixed signals and suboptimal performance.

What do you have to offer?

Based on your Purpose and your audience; what can you do for them? Why is it better than everything else on the market?

Are you:

- Making their life easier?
- Solving a problem that they have?
- Solving a problem that they do not know that they have?
- Making their life more exciting or entertaining?
- Helping them?
- Teaching them something?

What you have to offer is key to your brand message, and for the best result, it must be your **Unique Selling Proposition (U.S.P)**

A Tale on the U.S.P.

Let me get right down to it. USP stands for unique selling proposition (or unique selling point), and you must establish what yours will be right from the start.

Contrary to popular belief, a USP has nothing to do with logos, slogans, or graphic design.

Sure, those are components of your overall brand that help people identify your products and recognize you. However, a USP is far more important than that when building your customer base and breaking through the barriers of resistance that most businesses experience when they first appear in their market.

A USP is what truly tells potential customers how you are different from the competition. It helps to align your goals with your customers. Your USP tells them that you can be trusted, that you have their best interests at heart, and that you fulfill all promises. And most importantly, a USP ensures you aren't a faceless brand.

This would include key factors that differentiate a product or service from its competition, such as the lowest price, an extended, no-risk guarantee, a unique or exclusive product or offer not found anywhere else or the first-ever product of its kind.

Your USP should also demonstrate your dedication to satisfying customers and reassuring that you stand by your products and that there is no risk to your customer when doing business with you.

To start, think about what your product or service has that the competition doesn't.

Consider ways you can highlight those differences and emphasize the benefits. Paint a clear picture of why a prospect makes a wiser, sound decision to purchase your product instead of someone else's.

Your USP is the driving force behind the clearly illustrating value and giving potential customers a reason to purchase from you rather than the competition. That's one and only job.

Knowing how to develop a strategic brand message begins by recognizing what is already successful and improving on it within your own business.

You want to become the go-to person in your niche market, the obvious choice when customers consider who to turn to when making their purchasing decisions.

When you work towards building an unwavering presence in your market, starting with a strong foundation of trust, you'll immediately eliminate the barriers standing in the way of you connecting with your target audience. To achieve this, you need to learn as much as possible about them to capture their attention.

You'll also be able to lower the barrier of resistance and leave a lasting impression in their minds. When you do that, they'll come back to you time and time again.

Your Purpose, your audience, and your offer combined together make up your personal branding. The way you present and market yourself needs to reflect all three elements to make a positive impression on your consumers.

Once you have clearly defined all three of these, it is worth writing it all down somewhere. These make up the vision for your brand. You should check back in with these mission statements as your branding strategies progress to ensure that you are on the correct track.

You should be able to break them down to a few sentences, and it is recommended that you put them somewhere so you can refer back to it and be inspired by your personal branding — just as your future audience will be!

The Three Keys to the Success of a Credible Personal Brand: Audience, Authenticity, and Consistency

To be successful, you need to be credible. While there are a few ways to approach achieving credibility, the simplest ones are often the most effective. In this case, it is your audience, your authenticity, and realizing a level of consistency. Without these, you will not maximize the potential gains of your personal branding.

Your audience needs to trust you and, if your personal branding shows that you are authentic and consistent, they will.

Even though your audience will likely have never met you, effective personal branding makes it seem like they already know you — even though all that is really happening is that they are absorbing the content you are creating. Personal branding means that your audience will feel a bond with you; they will trust, respect, admire, and be happy to do business with you.

Audience

The importance of appealing to your clearly defined audience cannot be overstated.

The message of your brand is not going to appeal to everyone. You need to let go of the idea that everyone must like you for you to be successful. If you do not commit to a specific demographic of people, any message you create will not be as powerful. If you do not risk alienating people who are not part of your target audience, you risk not reaching those you want to.

Your personal branding needs to be attractive to your target audience. You could have the best branding, but it will be ineffective if it does not attract your goal audience. Your brand values need to align with your audiences, and the lifestyle you are trying to portray should share similar dreams with theirs.

This will be discussed in later chapters, but you need to put your brand where your audience will see it. You need to consider where they are, what they are looking for, and develop a content strategy that aligns with it.

Authenticity

Your personal branding needs to come across as authentic. With the rise of photoshop and influencer culture, consumers can tell when someone is showing a fake life — and they will tune out.

A "brand" does not mean a "persona." Instead, branding is a strategic showing of who you are.

Given how invasive and intertwined social media is with our lives and how easy it is to create a false impression, audiences want to follow someone real and authentic to who they are.

To achieve this, you should share parts of your story and be real with your audience. Sharing past experiences and future goals is a method that can be used to connect with your prospective consumer base — it should be done with caution; there is such a thing as oversharing!

Audiences do not naturally believe what they see or what is presented to them. They read reviews, look for multiple sources, and usually do not take things at face value. Having a strong personal brand is vital in narrowing this divide. If people trust you, if you seem authentic, passionate, and natural, they will engage with your content.

In this day and age, authenticity is currency; spend it wisely.

Consistency

We can discuss consistency in two ways. There is a more media-oriented level of professional consistency and then the engagement consistency.

The first of these is something that can very easily be achieved. It is so simple that it instantly stands out if it is missing from your personal branding and makes you seem unprofessional.

It is pivotal that, aesthetically, your content is consistent. This means ensuring you have good quality photos, a recognizable logo, and a unique design that makes you stand out. You should consistently use the same colors and fonts.

Again, this can take time to set up in the beginning but will have invaluable long-term results.

While we will discuss engagement more broadly later on, it is highly advised that you have a consistent content strategy. Creating quality content takes time. You do not have to rush out as much content as possible as quickly as possible. It is better to have fewer posts of a higher caliber than many posts that are low quality and put your audience off.

Having a consistent posting schedule of high-quality, relevant content will retain your audience and inspire them to engage with your posts.

Having strong personal branding requires accountability. You need to ensure that you are accountable, not only to your audience but also to yourself. Do not sabotage your brand by neglecting to maintain and monitor your strategies.

Put simply, the way to be seen as credible is to be reasonable.

Other Ingredients of a Credible Brand

The three keys to a credible brand have been mentioned above. But it will be best to treat other game players that knit the keys discussed above together, hence firm credibility or a killer brand. Let's get down to it.

A Focused Mission Statement

The strength of your brand begins with a specific and purposeful mission statement. This is the promise you make to your market, and it defines who you are and what you have to offer.

The easiest way to create a powerful mission statement is to think of your business from your customers' perspective.

Think about what motivates them to purchase products and how your business could persuade them so they feel that you're a credible and valuable partner in helping them achieve their goals.

A mission statement sets the tone for your entire brand story. It helps connect your products and services with your target audience by explaining exactly why they should purchase from you instead of your competitor.

If you struggle to create a mission statement for your brand, take a step back, and look at your business through the eyes of your average customer. Begin by outlining what you bring to the table and what you have to offer that sets you apart.

This doesn't mean you should include products or services in your mission statement; you definitely shouldn't. It simply means that you should be able to describe everything that encompasses your business using action-based words that build trust with your market.

Think of the value you bring to your market!!

How does your business provide a solution to a common problem in your market? How are you planning to stand out?

Your mission statement shouldn't be generic. It should apply specifically to your business and not some jargon that could be attached to countless other companies.

A Well-Designed Website

Whether you plan to sell products or services on your own or through third-party services like eBay, Shopify, or Etsy, you absolutely need to create a website of your own. Your website is the home of your brand. It's where you invite people so that they can get to know you, your business, and ultimately, where you serve them.

It's never a good idea to rely on third-party services if you value having control over your business. I've seen countless online merchants overlook the importance of having their own website.

What if they suddenly lose their Etsy, YouTube, or eBay account? What if something happens that costs them the only online presence they have?

Creating your own website puts you in full control of your brand, and it's a vital component in your long-term success.

That doesn't mean your website needs to be elaborate. It just needs to be functional and serve as a home base for your brand. You can work on growing it as you continue to build your business.

You can set up a cheap hosting account with www.BlueHost.com and have your website up and running in a matter of minutes using Wordpress. It doesn't have to be a difficult or time-consuming process. No excuses!

A Mailing List

It's important to begin growing your mailing list immediately. Do not put this off!

This is where your website comes into play. You should include a landing page with an opt-in form that connects visitors with your mailing list so that you can begin to grow your tribe. That way, you can easily reach out to your customer base and build valuable relationships with your audience.

Growing a list of subscribers who are actively interested in your niche is the easiest way to catapult your business to the next level. There is also no other marketing strategy that comes close to the effectiveness of a targeted mailing list, nor one as affordable.

You can get started with just a landing page that features an opt-in form and a mailing list account through services like www.Aweber.com

Choose a Differentiator

The single most important thing that will set your brand apart from any other is by having an obvious differentiator as part of your identity.

Here's a simple example of how a differentiator can be responsible for a brand's success, even in competitive markets where there are few ways to stand out.

A friend of mine writes romance. She publishes her stories on Amazon in what is a relatively crowded market. There are thousands of romance books published every week, yet she manages to generate over $15,000 a month in book sales.

The interesting thing is that her writing is no better than the majority of other books being published. She's also focused on mainstream romance niches rather than sub-genres.

So how does she manage to stand out and attract thousands of readers every month who have so many options to choose from?

Her brand is based on having the hottest book covers on the market. Despite her books being in an overly competitive market, her covers speak to potential readers and persuade them to one-click.

That's what her entire brand is based on. Having higher quality covers than the competition and staying up to date on the types of images that her audience best responds to.

She connects that with a slogan that identifies the type of books she produces. The tagline encompasses popular keywords that clearly define her brand: "Curvy Girls and Alpha Men." It's simple, but it's based on what she knows her readers want from a romance book.

Your brand needs a differentiator. Whether it's in the style of your website, the voice used throughout your content, or the quality of your graphics – your brand needs to offer something better than the competition. If all things are equal, there's no reason for someone to choose you over another offer, right? So, give them a reason to go to you.

Which Social Media will Best Benefit your Personal Branding?

There are so many different social media platforms in existence at the moment. It can be tempting to just join and post regularly on everything to reach the most amount of people. However, it is better to target your primary social media audience and build up from there.

Start smaller—claim domains, but creating content can be expensive and time-consuming, meaning you are better off investing in fewer mediums originally and growing as your audience does.

Before getting too carried away, you should research your industry and trends. Look at the popular accounts and posts; take note of what is similar and what is successful. Determine what the main characteristics are and figure out how to build on it differently. Researching your competition is essential in finding your content niche.

The most important thing to remember is to be consistent throughout your media; make sure it all uses the same branding, design, names, and all the information is up to date.

This section will provide a brief rundown on some of the most popular social media sites. Different sites work in various manners, but, most of all, remember to keep up with the trends.

A website

A website is an essential part of any personal brand. While it may be tempting to skip this platform in favor of social media, which tends to have higher user rates, a website is not an outdated concept! It is the perfect center of information for your personal branding.

You can use other platforms to share some of that information, but it is essential to have one, easy to navigate a place that consumers can access. It should, of course, have links to all your other social media profiles and contact information.

Facebook

Facebook is one of the biggest social media platforms in the world. Everyone is on it, which means you need to be careful about how you use it. Use a business page and attach it to a business profile account that aligns with your personal branding. Be active and share content from other platforms.

Being active on Facebook is vital — make sure that your page has a high response time, and you post regularly. Joining Facebook groups, "liking," and interacting with similar profiles are a great way to build up your audience.

Twitter

Twitter is an excellent way to connect with like-minded people, so make sure you follow all the relevant influencers and brands in your industry. Interaction is significant on Twitter; the best way to build up a following is to interact with other people's tweets, as well as posting your own.

Weigh-in on discussions that are relevant and use hashtags to reach a wider audience is one prowess of the twitter platform. Twitter threads are a great way to share some of your content, and do not forget to reply and interact with people who Tweet at you!

Instagram

One of the most popular photo-sharing websites is Instagram.

Instagram is also a good example of ensuring that you follow the trends. What once was a site where you could post random, overedited pictures of your friends has turned to a platform for people to carefully curate the best image of themselves possible—showing them success and having fun, effortlessly.

More recently, however, Instagram has seen a recent uptake in "carousels." These tend to be aesthetically laid out collections of information, written clearly in simple terms that get shared around. Before the middle of 2020, these were not really used. Instagram stories were not the place for ordinary people to share knowledge or quotes—for the most part. Now, however, the ways people use Instagram are changing; make sure you know this!

Pinterest

Pinterest can be seen as more of a niche social media site. People turn to Pinterest for inspiration, ideas, and step-by-step guides for achieving things. When uploading content to Pinterest, it should be artistic and visual, descriptions should be detailed, and any boards explicitly named, too.

Having a consistent and clear design on Pinterest is pivotal—else, your content will get lost in the clutter.

WordPress or other blogging platforms

Starting a blog is a good way to begin to create content for your audience. It is an easy method for you to start to share your personal branding. Using quality keywords, hashtags, and SEO is essential to get discovered.

Blogging about other people, tools, or events within your industry is a great way to get your content out there, so others have more of an inclination to share it.

Your posts should also be shared with other sites to increase traffic.

LinkedIn

LinkedIn is a social networking site for professionals. Having a detailed profile outlining your goals, business, and past experience is a fantastic way to add professionalism to your personal branding.

It is a platform full of like-minded people looking to make connections, grow their businesses, and further their careers. It is a great place to post your content.

YouTube

The biggest video sharing platform is YouTube, and many people use it to look for information. Videos are a great way to share your expertise; some audiences would rather watch than read.

However, it is important to remember that recording and editing high-quality videos can be time-consuming.

Podcasts

Podcasts are a newly popular medium. It is a very unique media type, and listeners often feel a real connection with the speakers. Audiences feel like they know and trust the hosts, even though they have never met. For this reason, podcasts are a great way to build an intimate connection with your audiences.

This was not an exhaustive list of all the social media platforms, just the major ones. There are many other sites out there, some with very niche userbases that could be perfect for your target audiences.

It is, of course, worth noting that different sites have different sharing abilities and having a following on Instagram, and then starting a podcast and using Instagram to promote, for example. The key to social media is simply to stand out, and to put your high-quality content on the right platforms is the easiest way to grow your following.

Irrespective of which platform you choose, your audience will only grow if you provide them with quality content.

Expand Your Business Reach Using Instagram

Using Instagram can be beneficial for all types of businesses. Whether you own a small hardware store or a high-end luxury boutique, Instagram is the perfect platform to help you market your products. This is because it provides your company with significant online exposure and appeals to your more visual audience, which leads to more sales conversions and profits.

Building on proven Instagram strategies helps to attract your targeted audience segments and increase your customer base. Small and medium-sized businesses sometimes shy away from using Instagram; however, trends have shown that Instagram works. With more traditional marketing mediums becoming less compelling to younger audiences, it's important to maintain a steady stream of new and/or young people to grow your business.

Some businesses believe that if you don't have a visually appealing product to showcase, Instagram is probably not worth the hassle, but that is the farthest thing from the truth. Businesses that sell services and products can all benefit from Instagram. The key is to push your brand more often than your products to gain greater brand recognition and influence on Instagram.

To remain relevant in today's ultra-competitive consumer world, successful businesses should find a way to attract the attention of audiences who are now looking to social media entertainment and content networks by creating traction through both proprietary media channels and earned media worth of mouth recommendations.

Compelling content that drives audience engagement is key. Posting with Purpose and having high-quality content can spark conversations and optimize engagement. Whether it's an expertly photographed image or a series of videos, content creation is the backbone of successful Instagram Business accounts.

However, engaging content is not enough to keep up with the business trends on Instagram. To properly leverage your account, you will want to engage with your customers and audience often. This can be through giveaways, contests, targeted campaigns, and other ideas.

Many businesses use Instagram instead of traditional advertisement space to make their followers aware of deals and sales they are hosting. It is also a powerful platform to capture leads and generate new revenue. In this guide, we will go over all of the best practices of establishing your small business on Instagram.

Instagram is a very visual platform, which is why compelling content is key to getting your followers to stop and read or view your post. There are many ways to do this, but the number one way is to always be authentic and genuine in your branding and message. What are your company's core values? What is a catchphrase associated with your company? What demographics does your company primarily serve? These are just a few of the questions you will want to ask yourself when taking your brand online to Instagram. Many of these factors have already been established, but your messaging needs to be tailored and curated for Instagram.

Generating Ideas for Posts

The best way to make sure you have Instagram content that resonates with your audience is to post relevant content and plan it out consistently. Some small businesses decide to hire a social media manager or social media planners that are already skilled in these areas. These specialists are creative and have experience creating words and imagery for brands to generate leads and sales. If you are not in the position to hire a social media planner just yet, you can give it a go yourself. It may take some experimenting to learn what captions and posts work best for your audience, but it is totally achievable.

Pick a theme based on your business or industry and create a brand guide that includes your company's logo, colors, and fonts. Creating unique branding can ensure that whenever your content is seen, people know just by viewing a post that it belongs to your company or brand. It's wise to learn and implement Canva, a simplified graphic design tool, as it will come in handy to create visually engaging images and graphics.

The best way to optimize your Instagram feed and plan what to post is to consider a website that schedules your content out over time. Whether it's two weeks or one month in advance, have an editorial calendar can be really beneficial and reduce the time spent to create posts.

There are thousands of social media management tools and schedulers for Instagram on the market, so deciding which one works best is all up to you. You may choose to start with one platform and then change direction based on new needs, and that is perfectly okay. Platforms such as Buffer, Hootsuite, Plann, and Later are some of the more popular options on the market today. These apps will help you visually layout your content and generate ideas of brilliant things for you to post. What to post:

The type of business you have will dictate what you post. Research the competition and like-minded companies to see what they're posting and the hashtags they are using to drive engagement. Use this as inspiration for what your content should like. What other businesses are in your industry or niche that are performing very well on Instagram?

If you are selling products, you could create quick 30 second tutorials on how to use them. If you are offering a service, you could create quotes and statistics about your industry to inform your audience of trends and current best practices. Memes are also pretty popular, and if you find some popular ones that are already created, that takes the duty of content creation out of your hands.

Videos are pretty popular on Instagram. Utilizing Instagram TV could give you a significant advantage as they are always on the Explore Feed of Instagram. Instagram is a fantastic way to connect with your audience and create expertise-like credibility with them.

Another great content idea is to create behind the scenes videos of your business, such as product creation or an in-depth look at your storefront, factory, or wherever your place of business is. Show your audience how ideas come to fruition, and you will gain their trust.

Whenever you are running promotions, sales, and deals, notify your audience by creating posts, whether it's a video or an image.

Using your existing customer's social media to showcase testimonials is also a great idea. Do you have repeat customers who are loyal to your brand that use Instagram? If they are not already posting about you, you should reach out to them and ask them if they are satisfied with your business. This brings us to our next point, which is influencers.

Many businesses turn to creative agencies that hire influencers and micro-influencers that are already using similar products or services and pay them to push and advocate for your brand. The word "influencer" includes a wide range of socially informed experts. Skincare, beauty, "foodies," and tech influencers, among others, will help businesses to accomplish what can be challenging demographics. According to Buffer.com, recent studies show that 70 percent of millennial consumers are influenced by their peers' recommendations for purchasing decisions on brands.

You could curate a press package and send it to influencers so that they can try out your product and give a review. User-generated content enables advertisers to share this information through social media accounts to build social proof and gain trust.

User-generated content is bringing real customers into the fold. This will increase your credit score, while consumers will be delighted to see their content shared or retweeted. Leveraging influencers and micro-influencers and featuring them on your feed and stories with product placement or services can help create authenticity and bridge the gap between your brand and a more extensive and steady audience.

Giveaways

If you implement it the right way, giveaways can help establish your Instagram account and brand, build loyal customers and an active audience who will share your incredible products or services with a broader audience than you can organically. Decide on what it is that you want to give away. Whatever the service, product, or experience you're giving away as your reward should be attractive to your audience. This will differ contingent on your goal. For example, if your goal is to spread awareness about a product launch, you should be most likely to give away the specific product as your reward.

Reaching out to other similar brands is also a great idea to cross-promote. Brand partnerships are especially helpful for younger, newer businesses. Aligning yourself with other reputable businesses and outlets can help to build your credibility. Move this process along by working with brands in your industry. Exchanging content or co-hosting an event and promoting it on Instagram and other social media platforms can push your businesses way farther than doing it alone. Your content will be twice as powerful with half of the effort.

Snapping Photos & Creating Videos

If you are creating content in house, there are tons of apps on the market that can help you start producing great photography and videos. Below we will outline some of the most popular apps and websites to help you jumpstart your Instagram content.

For high-quality photos:

Afterlight 2 is a pretty popular and powerful iOS-only photo editing solution. It's pretty affordable and offers a lot of tools to make the perfect edits. It's a flexible platform that works both for portrait shots and for capturing candid photos. Several filters are included, along with color and overlay capabilities.

Lightroom is a dependable mobile version of the much-loved Adobe suite platform. The application has a variety of presets that add a beautiful picturesque quality to your images. The free version is easy to use and has a sophisticated look, with color and lighting features that will take your Instagram photos to the next level. Even better, if you opt for the paid subscription option, you can unlock tons of more tools and features to enhance your images.

If you want to start creating video sooner than later, there is good news. There are thousands of mobile applications and web-based apps that exist now that can take your video to the next level. Good news: There are several free and inexpensive video editing applications and tools you can download that run from super simple to powerful in-depth abilities. Some of the more popular options are listed below:

Magisto is an online video editor with a web application and a mobile app for automated video editing and production for businesses and consumers. According to the website, Magisto uses Artificial Intelligence technology to make video editing quick and easy.

Inshot is an HD video editor that allows you to trim and cut video and movies, add music and video effects to stand out amongst the competition. It helps you create and edit videos with ease across multiple platforms, not just Instagram.

Hyperlapse is an application that allows you to create time-lapse photography, a method that enables your photographs to become motion pictures.

Optimizing Your Hashtags

Optimizing your hashtags is a great best practice to ensure that your relevant audiences are finding and following you. A host of websites and apps can help guide hashtags in a smart and manageable manner. When you use the right hashtags, you directly help Instagram organize and arrange your posts. This will help them reach people who value your products and your brand. It is important to know how to use them effectively.

There is a balancing act for using hashtags. You need to balance the ability to use common hashtags against the possibility of being squeezed out of trending and high-demand topics. This is similar to SEO in many ways. As you try to search for keywords in the Google search engine that are more generic, you will get more broad and generic results back.

Your business will do much better if you choose to rank for long-tail terms and curated hashtags. For example, if your business sells skincare products and solutions, using a hashtag such as #hyperpigmentation is more curated than going for an already very saturated hashtag like #skincareproducts or #beautyproducts. This directly targets an audience and consumers who may be looking for help with hyperpigmentation issues.

This is one of the main reasons why you need to provide some "long tail" hashtags in your posts. It will make it easier for your posts to compete with thousands, sometimes millions, of others using common hashtags. It is also wise to stay abreast of trending topics and use trending hashtags on your posts because it is current, and many people follow what's new and relevant.

In 2018 Instagram enabled the capability for followers to follow hashtags. This allows users to stay up to date on new posts that feature specific hashtags that they deem relevant to them. It is also wise for your business to follow specific hashtags to stay in the loop on the content generated, and it could help you identify new trends and inspire your feed.

Even websites and apps will help you generate the best hashtags to use based on your brand and show you how other competitors perform with those hashtags. Websites such as Ingramer.com and apps such as #HashMe are the perfect place to start if you need to get insight on what could work for your business.

The Instagram Algorithm

The long-debated concept of the Instagram Algorithm has seen much criticism since its inception. No longer are users seeing content from their closest friends and family first, but instead, they're shown a range of that the algorithm thinks they'd like the most. It used to be complex to understand, but to increase Instagram's transparency, Instagram released more details on this last year.

According to their latest reports, posts are prioritized based on the user's three key factors: interest, timeliness, and the relationship the user has with the accounts they are following. Understanding these trends can help Instagrammers to reach their desired number of Instagram impressions and followers.

Many experts have written articles and think pieces attempting to debunk the algorithm. Still, the main takeaways have been the same: Instagrammers who post consistently and engage with their audiences are always given priority on the timeline over other posts. This is important to note as you are building up your account on the platform.

The primary goal of Instagram is to increase the time that users spend on the platform. The longer the users stay, the more advertisements they display. So, directly or indirectly, the accounts that help Instagram achieve that goal will be rewarded.

Instagram Insights

Using Instagram's built-in insights is a huge benefit for accounts that are signed up as businesses. This tool gives you actionable information on how you can reach more people and meet your business goals. The feature has information on your followers' demographics, your most liked posts, your activity, and more.

It is wise to check this often to understand the times and dates your audience is online, and the type of content they engage with the most. You can also learn what actions people are taking once they click on your profile. If they decided to visit your website or clicked on your profile based on a post, you would know it by checking the insights. Knowing your best performing content can help you generate more ideas to produce similar posts instead of doing your own research and trying to come up with what you think is best.

The downside of Instagram analytics is that it only lets you see about a week's worth of growth from the app. To track your account's development with more detail and insights, you can use third-party apps and websites such as Later.com or PlannThat.com.

Building trust with your Instagram community

Businesses and marketing companies today face a massive challenge in trying to reach out to young consumers. According to a study conducted by executives from Crowdtap, Weight Watchers, and MRY, 84% of Millennials do not like or trust traditional advertising.

Building trust on Instagram is easy; just use the same methods and strategies you use in other areas. Your brand needs to have reputable products or services, and your message needs to be authentic. Share a clear, sharp vision of what your company stands for. This includes your company's core values, philosophies, and outlooks.

Social media and brand-loyalty go together, hand-in-hand. It's a modern method that helps brands engage emotionally by building trust with their consumer base. Pay careful attention to the type of content that engages users and focus on delivering it, and people will simply want to learn more about your brand.

To build a consumer-facing business, you need to use good marketing strategies and techniques. Businesses with a hazy stance on community concerns will not get very far when trying to attract new customers or sell to existing customers.

Customers want authenticity that they can relate to. Ensuring that you provide valuable content that solves a problem or answers a question is a great way to build up trust and increase audience retention.

Take communication to the next level by enabling consumers to post their photos and videos of their products on social media. Today, customers want real people to use the product before buying it themselves. The best way to get prospects and repeat customers to engage and follow you is to get in front of them and provide relevant information.

It's incredibly important to spend time on your own Instagram account and participate in other relevant sites. Consider sponsoring user-generated content to get your brand in the feeds of your customers. You can also hold an Instagram contest to bring attention to your brand while appealing to your target audience's slightly different segment.

Social media platforms foster two-way and group conversations. Use proven techniques to promote discussion and stay around to respond. Regramming and commenting on customer posts about your brand can also encourage brand loyalty.

Don't be spammy. What is this, you might ask? When the content you are posting or the comments you leave under other accounts don't appear authentic or meaningful. This is harmful because it usually results in people unfollowing you or engaging less with your own content.

You're probably eager to tell Instagrammers all about your excellent products or services. But before you post a glaring ad, take a break—social media users rate over-promotion as their top pet peeve. Don't break your audience's trust by being spammy. Pay close attention to the type of content that attracts users and focus on providing that, and people naturally want to know more about your brand.

Address negative feedback sooner than later

If you are running an Instagram business account, it's almost impossible to avoid getting negative feedback even if your products are the best first in class products around. Simply put, you just can't meet the expectations and demands of every consumer.

Customers are now flocking to social media platforms when they are dissatisfied, where they can complain about your product or service and get a response. It's easy to leave feedback on social media, as customers can reach you wherever they are. It is sometimes quicker than calling a customer service number and being put on hold or e-mailing a company for help to receive a response days later.

Consumers want and need to be heard, mostly when their business took-off from seeing a product on your Instagram for the first time. Instagram has become an important part of customer service, and selling your products is not enough to enhance authenticity. Even when a mishap or misunderstanding is not 100% of your company's fault, consumers almost always take the other consumers' side. Most small businesses do not have a Public Relations Specialist on hand that they can dial up in a crisis. It is best to address things quicker than later, even if you don't have all the facts prepared when it happens.

Recognize and acknowledge the customer's problem quickly. Don't wait until things snowball, and then other customers are alerted. This allows other customers to air their grievances with your company as well. You do not have to have another way. You really do not need a solution right away, but it is important to be transparent and open to what your customers have to say. The last thing you want is for the issue to go viral because you didn't take action soon enough or tried to ignore the problem.

It is also important not to address every hostile third party that might chime in or have no business with your company at all. The internet calls these people "social media trolls." These people just want to join in on the conversation and stir up trouble for its fun. It is important to discern between genuine dissatisfaction in your customers and those who get a kick out of it trolling.

When you finally do come to a resolution, there is nothing wrong with doing a PSA of sorts to let the rest of your audience know that an issue has been handled. This will help reaffirm their trust in your brand and confirm that your company is proactive when mistakes do happen.

Brands that have successfully used Instagram

There are hundreds of businesses and brands that are successfully executing Instagram campaigns and have case studies you can learn from. Instagram is growing larger each day, and it is one of the go-to platforms and best places for businesses to invest in ad space. From smaller startups to the largest global brands, everyone uses Instagram in some shape or form to boost their business. Below we will outline some of the most notable business case studies, which use it effectively, and their results.

Adidas #MyNeoShoot

As one of the top brands in apparel and footwear, Adidas has utilized social media marketing to surpass its competition. In 2018 Adidas executed a campaign called #MyNeoShoot. To promote its Neo brand, which launched in 2012.

The Neo brand was a new subset division of Adidas geared towards trendy, youthful consumers. They invited their followers to create Adidas-inspired Instagram posts with the hashtag and labeling them with the hashtag #MyNeoShoot. They then asked the best content creators to model in a professional photoshoot and shared their branded photos with engaging social media followers and Adidas's own accounts. They even recruited Selena Gomez to help with the contest.

As a result, the campaign generated 71,000 mentions of the #MyNeoShoot for Adidas. The hashtag also enabled them to gain 41,000 new followers. This was a splendid example to show that a creative contest is enough to engage your viewer and underscore social media influencers' importance.

Old Spice

The Old Spice brand is somewhat known for its reputation for its clever and quirky ad campaigns, but sometimes credibility can be more of a burden than a reward. How does Old Spice stay at the forefront of edgy advertising? How do you create engaging marketing assets when your target audience already has clear expectations for you to be creative? The answer for Old Spice was to focus efforts into unknown territory: social media with their Dream Runner Campaign.

In 2016, Old Spice introduced The Dream Runner campaign. The campaign encouraged their followers to win things by posting photos of their running routes in the shape of a prize they wanted to win – complete with the hashtag #runoldspice.

Using the thousands of apps out there, runners tracked their daily runs and highlighted the routes they took across the different cities to win prizes. Their campaign motto was, "If you can run it, you can own it." It was a case study of how to use your audience's favorite activities and interests to boost your campaign.

Once again, this campaign showed how prominent Instagrammers played a significant role in helping Old Spice hit their campaign goals. It's also a great example of reducing marketing pressure by selecting influencers that already fit the brand's ideals to promote the brand and their products that would be enjoyed by most people exposed to the advertisement.

Camp Brand Goods
Camp Brand Goods is a good example of a smaller company getting in on the Instagram trend. Their brand is inspired by the outdoor and travel niche and lifestyle.

According to Business.com, the brand created the #keepitwild contest, which awarded a weekly t-shirt to users who posted the most original photo with this hashtag. They ran this contest to increase their followers and increase engagement. During the competition, the company partnered with other Instagram users known in the outdoor world and helped them attract more followers.

Monetizing Strategies to Drive Sales

Instagram has now added the ability for qualified, eligible businesses to tag their products in posts. This practice is called "shoppable media." Customers can get details about your products from your posts and purchase them.

Once you have enabled shoppable post, customers can click on the link directly from Instagram, and it will take them to a checkout page on your whatever landing page or e-commerce website you have your products on. To do this, you will also need a Facebook for a Business account to set up a catalog of your products. Unfortunately, this isn't available for business selling services, but there are other ways to connect your services through Instagram.

Utilizing Instagram stories is great for both businesses selling products and services. If you have Instagram businesses, account over a certain following, you can advertise to consumers directly from your stories and enable a call-to-action for them to swipe up to view more about whatever it is that you are selling.

Use this guide to learn how to start executing your Instagram strategy properly. All-in-all focus your efforts on the solutions you deliver to your customers and not just the products. Instagrammers want to know how your brand and products can provide value to their everyday life.

Create a consistent voice for your brand and reliable and consistent information. View your Instagram Business Account from behind the scenes to gain insight into how viewers might perceive yours. It could help to have a trusted friend or colleague look at your content and strategies to see if they resonate with non-stake holders.

You may think it's better to be broader with your messaging to gain more followers, but the more niche-related your tactics are, the better the conversion of followers into actual buyers. Keeping your customers interested is a vital part of any successful marketing campaign. Don't underestimate the potential value that Instagram has to grow your business.

Strategies to Grow your Personal Brand and Authority

Once you have decided on your medium, there are a few different methods that you can use to grow your brand and authority.

Having strong personal branding positions you as an authority, and your content will reflect this, too.

Creating Content

The best way to grow your personal branding is to create content. Creating your own quality content is the best method to show that you are an expert, trustworthy, and deserve your audience's time.

It works best if you curate content specifically for the medium you are primarily posting on. However, posts can also be shared with other platforms for increased visibility.

Getting involved in Facebook groups is a great way to interact with your audience more casually. Direct, personal interaction will make them trust and respect you. Once you have enough of an audience, you could also start your own Facebook group for your content.

Instagram posts, blog posts, and videos are all fantastic ways to grow your branding. But, of course, quality is better than quantity. Post as much valuable content as possible and try to include a call to action for your audience.

Your content does, of course, need to be unique. It should reflect your personal branding, your values, and your goals; and speak to your target audience in such a way that they feel compelled to act.

Mailing List

Email marketing is a super effective method of connecting with your audience. Create links and leads in your other content and make it easy to subscribe, so any future content gets sent straight to their inbox.

A weekly newsletter can be a super-effective way to connect with your audience. You can include personal on-brand anecdotes and link back to posts you have made over the week to remind your audience to engage with your posts.

Offering an incentive to subscribe to your mailing lists, such as discounts on your paid content, sneak previews on future content, or exclusive new content, will help your audience feel included in your personal branding and encourage engagement.

Free Content

Offering free content and resources allows your audience to see that your content will be of a high caliber. It builds trust and ensures that the audience is aware that the paid content will be of premium quality.

Audiences are usually more likely to pay for full access to a product or service if they have had a positive experience with a free preview.

Smaller Professional details are Key

Small details are key in proving that your personal branding makes you a credible and reputable voice in your industry. This includes professional headshots (consistent across platforms), acceptable language and proofreading, design, aesthetic consistency, and even an email signature. These are such small elements that immediately make you an authoritative source of knowledge.

Creating Proper Connections Within your Industry

A great way to bring exposure to your personal branding is to reach out to other people in your industry or similar key players.

Being featured on a popular and well-respected platform in your industry will elevate your credibility and authority.

It can be worth reaching out to other brands and seeing if they need features or guest blogs—this syndicates your brand's credibility as it shows that other trustworthy and prominent sources value your work.

While it can seem tempting to build your personal branding alone, such connections and collaborations are an invaluable way to reach different aspects of your audiences.

Gain Instant Brand Authority with Storytelling Campaigns

Storytelling can be a powerful component in a marketing strategy. It can be the driving force behind developing, and more importantly, establishing a brand that connects and resonates with your target audience.

The story you tell and the method in which you use to weave that story throughout your marketing campaigns will be based on your overall goals, but one thing remains the same:

Your story will be structured to introduce your brand to the world in a way that helps you stand out and apart from the competition.

Storytelling is a testament to our hard work; it highlights the efforts we've taken to create a distinctive brand, and it helps deliver larges pieces of content in a way that people can connect to.

It's also the easiest way to express emotions and illustrate your commitment to providing value.

There's nothing more potent than a carefully crafted story that fulfills the needs of your core market.

In this special report, we'll cover the top story-telling methods, how to best use these strategies, and how you can use storytelling to strengthen your brand or launch a new one.

Without further delay, let's begin!

The Art of Storytelling

Content marketing is when you figure out ways to utilize and repurpose content so that a broader audience sees it. Storytelling and content marketing go hand-in-hand.

With storytelling, you can design a highly-engaged marketing campaign that carries a strong focus. You'll use storytelling to give people the information they want to hear to make the decision to follow your brand, purchase your products, or connect with your platform.

Thankfully, there's an easy structure to creating a compelling storyline for your marketing campaign, and it begins with utilizing a variety of delivery methods, including:

Visual and Content-Based

Visual storytelling would include videos, presentations, Webinars, or perhaps a series of episodes that bring your viewers seven on a journey.

Content-based would include everything else, such as articles, blog posts, sales pages, and so on.

It's essential to combine both storytelling methods into your marketing campaigns so you're able to reach a broader audience. Some people prefer to watch a video; others absorb information better in text form.

The anatomy of a successful storytelling campaign will also include a specific series of questions and answers. We'll dive deeper into this in the next chapter, but for now, here's a quick overview of what you need to consider when designing your storytelling campaign.

Questions from your Audience

This isn't where you poll your market for their most burning questions, though that can be an effective strategy in coming up with a storyline that connects with your core audience. But another way to address questions without surveying your market begins with the questions you had when you first ventured into your niche.

Look at what questions your customers are already asking? What answers your competitors are providing? And how best to connect with your audience using language they best understand.

Establishing a Timeline

This is where you draft your story arc around a marketing campaign. This story will tell your audience how you got from point A to B, why you created your brand (services/products), and how it exists to serve them.

It gives your story purpose and helps you stay aligned with your goals while remaining consistent with your campaigns. Laying the groundwork for a storytelling timeline is also important so that you're able to.

Personalization

Your story needs to connect with your core audience, and you do this by making it all about them. Rather than creating a generic storyline that simply highlights your brand, you need to embrace your audience by fostering a mindset that you understand what they need, desire, and fear.

And finally,

Adaptation

One story doesn't fit all marketing channels, so you need to make sure you create stories that align with the platforms you use.

For example, suppose you plan to utilize social media. In that case, you'll want to begin by uncovering key themes, trends, and in-demand topics within those channels and then create a storyline around what has proven to be effective.

Facebook marketing is different than Instagram marketing, and they cater to specific audiences, so you'll want to customize your storyline to fit those viewers better.

Instead of going straight for sale, you need to think about how people communicate on those platforms, recommend products and services, and how the market responds to different ad styles. Then you can create your own storytelling campaign so that it aligns with those networks.

In the next section, we'll talk about how the three key points of every successful storyline. This is how you structure a story so that it goes the distance in connecting with the heart of your audience.

Stories that Sell

Every story has three main parts: the beginning, the middle, and of course, the end. When using storytelling to further your outreach, your story needs to cover all the bases, which means you'll begin by:

Step 1: Setting the Stage

In the first part of your storytelling campaign, you're essentially laying the foundation for your story arc. You're setting the scene.

In phase 1, you're outlining the conflicts that your audience is suffering from. In other words, you're acknowledging the problems that they need help with and clarifying your brand message to demonstrate you understand your market and what they're struggling with.

This is an important step because it will set the tone for your entire campaign and help connect your brand with its audience.

Step 2: Providing a Solution

In the second part of your storytelling campaign, you're offering your audience with a solution to the problems outlined in step one.

You're connecting with your market by being personal, engaging them directly with your content, and demonstrating that you understand what they need and can give it to them.

Step 3: Call to Action

At the end of every great romance book, the hero and heroine ride off in the sunset, finally at the point of living happily ever after. In market-based storytelling, you're promoting your customers to click that buy button, subscribe to your channel, or follow your brand so they can achieve that same happily ever after.

This is where they need to decide to move forward and set themselves on the path towards reaching their goals with your help and guidance.

The anatomy of every successful story always includes these three crucial steps. Launching a storytelling campaign with a hard sell or an aggressive approach that bypasses steps one and two will result in turning away many customers who would otherwise fall in love with your brand.

You need to romance them throughout your campaigns. This begins by explaining that you understand their issues, provide a solution to that conflict, and then prompt them to take action to experience the rewards.

In the next section, we'll look at how personal stories can help infiltrate the most competitive markets and help you stand out in crowded spaces.

How to Inspire & Motivate

Stories must carry a level of inspiration and motivation, and there's no easier way to do that than by making it personal.

This is where you explain why your brand was created, what motivated you to create a company in your market, and your personal goals and missions.

Of course, you want to keep your audience in mind when crafting this story to feel a part of it and go on the journey with you.

For example, if you are selling a weight loss course designed to help people live a better, healthier life, your story should begin by outlining your personal journey and transformation.

You become your own case study and, subsequently, the best testimonial you can possibly offer.

But you then need to emphasize how your training program will produce the results your audience is looking for. It's one thing that you could accomplish your weight loss or fitness goals, but how can others be sure they can follow your lead?

This is where personal storytelling becomes a critical component to successfully connecting with your audience on a deep level. It's when you get the opportunity to show them what's possible and how by purchasing your fitness program, they too will be able to reach their goals.

The more personalized your storytelling campaigns are, the more effective they'll be. Testimonials are a powerful weapon in sales and marketing. Still, when you begin by sharing your own personal journey with your audience, you'll be able to create an unforgettable story that will motivate and inspire your audience.

In the next section, I'll share some tips and techniques to maximize your storytelling campaigns' effectiveness.

Effective Storytelling Hacks

I call these storytelling hacks because they're fast and easy ways to ensure you are hitting the hot buttons and fulfilling your goals by creating an irresistible story that will resonate with your audience.

Tip 1: Listen to your Audience

Once you've kicked off your storytelling campaign, you need to start listening. This is when you gauge responses and keep a pulse on how your audience feels about your story.

Listening to responses helps you tweak your storyline so that it better aligns with what your market is looking for, so you must stay on top of each phase of your storytelling campaign and leave room for adjustments and growth.

Tip 2: Be Memorable

This goes without saying, but there are easy ways to ensure your story is share-worthy. You want to get as many people talking about your story as possible, which means you want to research and understand audience triggers and overall motivations. Knowing your audience will make it easier for your stories to stick.

Tip 3: Be Personal

You want your story to connect with the average consumer in your market, so it needs to be made simple to enhance understanding.

Getting personal in your storytelling campaigns will make it easier for you to connect with your market. Still, it will also ensure you're approachable, come across as genuine, and that you are deeply involved.

People want to know that you are offering a high level of engagement and involvement in the products and services they purchase.

It's all about creating a marketing campaign that improves the experience of your customers.

Tip 4: Be Relatable

I just mentioned the importance of personalizing your campaigns, but you want to take things a step further by ensuring you are reliable. It's easy to look at our market as groups of people without understanding the kind of audience we're catering to.

What makes them tick? What are they most interested in? What do they fear? What are their overall goals?

Being relatable shows them that you've done the job of researching the market to know what is most important to them, but more importantly, it demonstrates that you've worked hard to create a brand that's tailored to their needs.

I wish you the very best with your storytelling campaigns!

The Importance of Analytics

Now that you have decided on your target audience, the platforms you will be using to share it, and its content, it is essential to track its progress.

Analytics can be confusing to understand initially, but once you are familiar with them and how they benefit you, they will allow you to fine-tune your content and post and maximize your personal branding returns.

In short, analytics can help you track how well your posts are doing. You can use them to check various details to verify that your content reaches your target audience and meets your branding goals.

Checking your analytics allows you to monitor, reflect, and recreate your personal branding's success—and may help you catch any shortcomings early on.

Intense growth does not always happen overnight, and it can be unrealistic to go viral immediately. But, by tracking your progress, you can capitalize on your personal branding's successes as they happen.

Engagement

Engagement is a two-way street. The first form of engagement is audience engagement. Engagement occurs not when your audience views your post, but when they like it, comment on it, share it and take action from it.

Most platforms have built-in insights and engagement checking functionality.

You can see the demographic breakdown of your followers (to make sure you are reaching your target audience), as well as the number of likes. One of the most important forms of engagement is the number of people who have seen the most versus the number of people who have taken action from it (including likes, shares, and comments). If you have many viewers but low actions, your content is resonating with your audience.

Alternatively, if your posts are not being seen, consider changing your content schedule. Make sure you are posting when your audience is active and include a call to action in your content.

The other form of important engagement is your own. Are you regularly checking your accounts, responding to comments, replying to questions, or just otherwise interacting with your audience?

This makes your branding accessible, credible, and authentic. You want your audience to feel like they can trust you, and when you are online, you are available.

Keyword planning and Search Engine Optimization

Search engine optimization and keyword planning, in essence, just make you more easily found when audiences search for relevant things to your brand.

Planning out keywords is a good step to take when trying to reach your audience. Use words relevant to your personal branding and industry, making sure you check for popular words and phrases.

The popular and common searches do change over time, so ensure that you keep up with the trends. Audiences also change their word searches depending on the satisfaction with the results — so try and keep synonyms in mind.

Search Engine Optimization (SEO), while similar to keyword planning, prioritizes better quality content.

Search engines rank search results, and the higher up in the results you are, the more credible and more trustworthy you will seem. How many times, really, do you go to the second page of results?

Tailoring your personal branding to be optimized for search engines is a perfect way to show your audience that you are credible.

Search engine optimization is an organic way of gaining traffic to your profiles and naturally growing an audience.

Public Image

When you search for yourself online, what comes up? Do you have a common name and get lost in a crowd of other people? Do old posts you made come up? Do you even come up at all?

You should take the time to search for yourself and be thorough! Check your names, and add extra words, including schools, locations, associates, family members, and workplaces. You need to know exactly what is out there. Clear your browsing data, use incognito mode, and even get other people to search for you too.

If a drunken picture of you posted on Facebook shows up before a professional headshot when you image search, you may have a problem! Remove any controversial posts that you are tagged in or weird party pictures you uploaded as a teen.

If a potential customer searches for you and sees things that do not align with the personal branding you have created, they may take their business elsewhere.

Some other tips for improving search results

As you know, when you search for something, multiple results show up. Try and improve and optimize your SEO to rank highly and take up more of the popular results.

When creating profiles, make sure you use the same name on all of them. Try to get the same username if possible. Make sure to include your location and fill out all the relevant information.

If you want to have personal accounts for your friends and family only, separate to your business accounts, consider using a different name, and put the privacy settings on high. If personal accounts are discovered to not align with your personal branding, it will make you seem inauthentic and discourage audiences.

Ways to Live your Personal Branding and Increase Visibility

Now that the digital footprint element of personal branding creation has been summarized, we will now take our journey off-screen.

It is not enough to just have a good media strategy that portrays your brand in one way and then act differently in your everyday life. Of course, you can do this; however, should your audience come into contact with this alter-ego, it can be confusing and makes your personal branding weaker and less trustworthy.

Your personal branding is the combination of who you are, what you do, and what you want to do. Everything you do is associated with your brand, and this includes your everyday life.

Build a Network

One of your aims should be to build a network of connections with other key players in your industry. Being friends with successful people makes you appear like one of them.

If you know people and come up in suggested searches or tagged posts, not only is it easier for your audience to find you, but other industry players will likely find you, too. Having a network makes it easier for different media types looking for some to feature to connect with you and share your brand with their audience.

Often, people with brands similar to yours will look for experts to share insights with their audience, so you can harness these opportunities by having such connections.

Collaborations are often mutually beneficial; so, you should be on the lookout for interviews or guest blogging positions to help you reach more consumers in your audience.

Being seen with reputable and credible brands make you appear so, too.

Aside from networking platforms such as LinkedIn (as well, of course, as other digital media locations), you can increase your network's size by attending conferences and industry events.

Remember, it does not matter what you know; the important part is who you know. And you never know who might hold the next big opportunity for you.

Build an Accessible Community

As well as having a good network of industry connections, it is also important to have an accessible community for your audience. For your personal branding to be successful, you need your audience to trust and respect you; they will do this if they feel like you are a real person, not just a businessperson!

Your audience will want to connect with you as a person, not a nameless, faceless avatar.

There are a few ways to build up a "community" around your personal branding. This can include holding in-person events to meet up with your audience or, at the very least live sessions.

Starting a Facebook group (and being active in it) is a great way to get a discussion going and impart your wisdom on a personal level. Even just responding to comments on your content posts is a great way to be seen as reachable and available.

You should also make sure you have contact options for your audience; this includes emails and messages. You should monitor your comment section so that you are up to date with how your audience is responding to your content. Remember that many social media platforms showed when you were last active or show how responsive you are to messages; make sure you are keeping response times down to show that you care and are available.

At the end of the day, people connect with people; the value of genuine human connection cannot be overstated.

Business Cards

So maybe business cards seem like an outdated concept, but they can be useful to invest in. You can hand them out to new business associates or simply pass them on to people when you meet them—but in a professional manner, of course.

Some of the benefits of business cards include the fact that they are an easy way to give someone all your details in one convenient place. If you include all your social media handles and other ways to contact you, your audience will be able to reach you in their preferred manner.

Business cards are a fantastic physical reminder of your personal branding— it is harder to lose a piece of paper than to forget details.

The design and branding on your business card should be consistent with your digital footprint—this means matching fonts, logos, and other aesthetic staples of your brand.

Dressing Well

Your personal appearance should match the brand that you have created. You are the physical embodiment of your branding, so you need to have a look that matches the brand. Dressing well is the best way to achieve this— it makes you look trustworthy and professional. You do not need to be in a three-piece suit always, but taking pride in your appearance shows that you take pride in your brand.

Share your Story

Your audience wants to do business with a person. Sharing your story brings down the walls between businessperson and human.

You should share the story behind your brand with your audience. Show them why you are passionate, how you are qualified, and what you want to achieve. You could incorporate this into your content strategy or even just include an "about" page on your website.

Humanizing yourself and sharing your life story, including hardships you overcame and what inspired you to become the person you are, will build a strong connection with your audience. It adds a level of authenticity and will make your audience believe in you and your personal branding.

If it would suit your branding strategy or content schedule, you should share elements of your day with your audience. This is not essential, but it is a way of building a connection with your audience. Including your day's insights, even something as simple as getting a morning coffee resonates with people and shows that you are serious about your personal branding.

Of course, there is such a thing as oversharing. You need to seem open, and upfront yet maintain a degree of separation. Decide on what the appropriate level of sharing is that will foster a real connection with your audience. Once they are engaged and feel like a part of your life, they will be more likely to participate with your branding in the future.

In essence, you need to ensure that your actions and lifestyle align with the image you want to convey with your branding. Carrying aspects of your branding with your everyday life will create authority in your work. It shows that you are serious and credible—that your vision for yourself is a reality and not a scheme to make money. Your audience wants to know that you care, both about them and about your branding. Living your brand is the best way to accomplish this.

Recurring Income Strategies

If you're looking to boost your income, grow a loyal following and position your brand as the go-to source in your market, there is no easier way than injecting a recurring revenue stream into your business.

With recurring revenue, you can create a strong foundation for your business while taking advantage of the opportunity to incorporate additional income streams into an ever-growing community.

Not only will you profit from the regular subscriptions, but you can utilize a series of proven strategies to skyrocket sales of other products and services! Plus, recurring revenue is consistent and predictable. Unlike other income streams, such as with one-off products or services, you know what to expect with a monthly or yearly recurring revenue platform.

You aren't bouncing from one product launch to another. Instead, you can focus on growing your community and extending the value of your program. Instead, you are focused on a scalable business and stop trading your time for money. This special report will show you exactly how to join the recurring revenue revolution and how it can work in almost any niche or market.

You'll also discover how to choose a format that focuses on long-term success so you can enjoy the benefits of passive income every month - all on complete autopilot. And that's just one of the many advantages of incorporating a stream of recurring income into your business.

Not only are you able to keep payments rolling in every cycle, but you can set it up so that it works towards driving in customers every single day, all within one platform.

Plus, it's always easier to sell to existing customers than it is to convert new ones. Are you ready to begin? Let's get started!

Recurring Revenue Streams

You've seen the rise of recurring revenue streams in your everyday life. Blockbuster fell victim to Netflix; cable TV fell victim to online streaming services like Amazon Prime.

Everywhere you turn, companies are focused on building multi-million dollar businesses on the recurring income platform.

Even brick and mortar businesses have jumped on the bandwagon by creating loyalty programs where people can pay for a certain amount of services a month (drink packages, spa treatments, car wash services, express mail delivery services, etc.)

In fact, virtually every business can benefit from adding a recurring revenue stream. There's no doubt about it; now is the time to get in on the action.

To start, it's important to come up with a primary benefit for your recurring income stream.

- Why would people want to sign up for your program?
- What are the benefits?
- How is it different from others?

For example, with a spa package, someone could purchase a $100 package that gives them the ability to book three massage treatments, rather than the usual 2.

With an online business, you could offer access to advanced training or exclusive resources not available anywhere else. The key is to highlight the benefits upfront. Customers sign on for recurring programs because they get more money for their buck or are given access to something unique, special, and exclusive.

Or, perhaps they are looking to save time or alleviate an otherwise steep learning curve.

In some businesses, the draw is that subscribers belong to a tribe or a community such as fitness programs or yoga studios. The same holds true with online programs that incorporate private groups and forums where people can network and encourage one another.

Regardless of the format you choose, you need to develop a clear benefit that will persuade people to sign on and stay subscribed. In the following chapters of this special report, we'll look at some of the most popular recurring revenue business models so you can choose one that works best for you.

Membership Programs

Subscription-based programs are not only extremely profitable, as they generate recurring income, but they are single-handedly one of the easiest ways to gain traction in your market and position yourself as an expert in your field.

With a membership program, people sign up for ongoing access to exclusive content. This is where they become part of your community and are often given the option to network with others or ask questions via a private group or forum as they progress through the training. You've likely seen this in action for yourself when you've signed up for a course or training program. The course instructor has positioned themselves as an expert on the topic by providing a clear, workable system to accomplish a specific goal or task.

By providing step-by-step training in a specific niche, you will be able to secure your foothold in your market and become a leading source for quality information.

In other words, you become the go-to person in your field. They are phenomenal at increasing your customer outreach, maximizing exposure, and managing a sales funnel so that you can leverage your ever-growing community.

Another great thing about the membership model is that you can create a flagship program geared towards helping your subscribers learn about one topic and then work towards expanding your program as your community grows to keep subscribers moving through your sales funnel.

There are many ways to build a successful membership program. Begin by considering the commonly asked questions in your niche. Perhaps someone needs help with graphic design. Rather than spending all your time teaching people how to master a specific software program on a one-on-one basis, you could create a membership site that offers access to video training that shows them how to use a third-party product to enhance their business.

Then, not only are you generating recurring income from your own training program, but you are also able to make money via affiliate marketing.

You can package your membership program in many ways, including by offering tutorials, resources, coaching, community access, or a combination of them all.

There are a few popular models used to create membership websites, including:

Evergreen Content Model

This is where your content is released in the same sequence regardless of when someone joins your program. For example, someone who joins in January would receive access to the first month's content immediately. Then in February, they would receive access to the second month's content and so on.

A member who joins in February would still receive January's content as month 1. Every member starts at the beginning of your content cycle and then progresses as the months go on.

With an evergreen content system, the content is released sequentially based on each customers' join date.

These are often the easiest membership sites to set up because you can create the content once and then set & forget.

The only downside to this format is that you may struggle to offer group coaching as students will be at different stages of your training.

Current Month Access

This type of membership platform is based on the current month. Someone signing up in January would receive access to that current month's content.

If someone signed on in February, they would only gain access to that current month's content. So, every member is given access only to the latest update. You can further monetize this membership site style by giving members the option to purchase access to archived content separately.

This model helps to increase every customer's value because they are purchasing access to current content while purchasing additional access to unlock prior months or advanced content. This format works well if your content is segmented so that each month's content can stand alone and isn't dependent on previous lessons or training.

All-Access Pass (Content Buffet)

This format usually involves providing members with access to all previous content and new content monthly as long as they are a paid member.

Typically, you can price these membership programs at a higher price point because subscribers gain access to all the available content, regardless of when it was released.

Programs that run this way would include programs like https://www.Lynda.com, where you pay for access to their training database and then browse through their full library of courses and training material that continues to grow. Consider the different formats available so you can determine what would work best for your target market.

For example, the weight loss market is a popular one for membership programs (example: Weight Watchers) because their monthly program guides someone through their journey from the very beginning until they've reached their weight loss goals.

Their monthly membership never ends either because even when someone finally reaches their goal weight, they are then transferred into a membership program designed to help them maintain their weight.

And another valuable part of their community is in the groups and forums members gain access to. They can find an accountability partner, personal online trainers, and coaches in these areas that help them stay on track.

With this type of platform, you cannot only generate income monthly from the recurring membership fees, but you could easily expand your membership program to offer an additional upgrade. The additional upgrade includes access to weekly meal plans, community support, fitness strategies, and customized weight loss plans.

Regardless of the membership format you choose, you'll want to make sure you use a platform that supports your goals.

You should look for a membership software solution that offers quick-setup, a user-friendly admin panel, security, and of course, flexibility regarding content options as well as payment processors.

I personally recommend ProductDyno, available at https://www.ProductDyno.com

ProductDyno works for all digital product formats, including the ability to sell monthly content in whatever format you choose, as well as the ability to sell licenses to software, themes, designs, or plugins.

The admin panel is intuitive, and they offer prompt support and regular updates so you can rest assured you're given access to in-demand features. It's simply one of the easiest ways to get your membership site off the ground with minimal cost and effort.

Bonus Tip: Once you have your membership program off the ground, you could offer personalized coaching access to a small group of students. You could choose to offer this only once a year when you have time or offer it on an ongoing basis.

Coaching is a premium service, which means that you'll be able to set a higher price point than other types of services. It's a great way to inject additional cash flow into your existing community.

Software Products(SaaS)

SaaS stands for *Software as a Service* and is offered on a subscription basis.

The benefits are quite obvious to customers: in exchange for their recurring payments, they are given the ability to use the software while knowing that it is updated regularly and that they'll gain access to prompt customer support. From DropBox and Adobe to mailing list providers like MailChimp and Aweber, many of the leading brands have incorporated SaaS into their businesses and, for a good reason, drastically increases their yearly income it easier for them to provide value to their customer base.

Not ready to create your own SaaS product? No problem! You can still build recurring income in this industry by promoting useful products and services that your customer base could benefit from.

For example, perhaps you run a community focused on teaching people how to build a successful blow. You could create a training program that teaches them how to launch a successful website while promoting the tools they need to get the job done.

This might include SaaS-based mailing lists, hosting for their blog, or perhaps design and graphic tools, as well as plugins. The possibilities are endless when it comes to making money, promoting a variety of recurring revenue products.

There are dozens of important tools you can easily promote within your own content to generate revenue.

And for every new customer you send their way; you'll earn a recurring income from their ongoing payments. Win-win!

Physical Product Subscription

You've likely heard of the Dollar Shave Club as well as other subscription boxes that focus on health, fitness, or cosmetics, just to name a few. These are growing in popularity every single day.

Here's how it works:

Customers subscribe to a service, and in exchange, they receive a box of products every month. The products vary but are usually all in the same niche or industry.

This format works well because recipients not only look forward to receiving new products every month in the mail, but they become part of a community of active users.

Most product-based subscription sites host groups and forums where people can discuss the products and share feedback. Cosmetic lines promote their subscription boxes by asking users to upload photos of them using their products. They create tutorials based on the different cosmetics included in the monthly offering.

The downside is that creating a physical product subscription program isn't always the easiest business to launch. It will require coming up with products and packaging and shipping and distribution partners, but don't overlook the possibilities. There may be a way to simplify the program so that it works for your business.

For example, an author who self-publishes books via Amazon KDP could create a subscription program where readers can sign on to receive a new book every month via their exclusive book club.

While an author may not release a new book every month, they could easily send out some of their favorite reads, promoting other up-and-coming authors. The shipping costs would be minimal, and it could even be automated through sites like Lulu.com.

How could you incorporate a physical product subscription into your business?

It's time to put that thinking cap on and see how you could take advantage of this profitable opportunity! **Tip:** You could also combine a membership program with a physical product subscription plan.

For example, you could sell access to an online training program that offers guides, tutorials, and videos and provide them with a physical copy of the course via a book.

Online Courses

While courses don't usually bring in recurring income on their own since many are designed on a platform that involves a student paying a one-time fee for access to the training, you can still generate consistent recurring revenue by focusing on a **strong front-end sales funnel** that directs students to other products and services.

For example, while your course may be a one-time charge, you could give students the option to upgrade to a monthly membership that offers tools and resources associated with the training program's topic.

This could include additional auxiliary components such as webinars, printable downloads, or additional workbooks that go beyond your course scope.

Start by thinking about a topic for your course and the content formats you would feel comfortable creating.

This could include:

- Text-based lesson plans
- Video Tutorials
- Webinars
- Interviews with Experts
- Workbooks and Customized Lesson Plans
- Printables (checklists, guides, etc.)

The key is to identify an ongoing demand for help with specific problems. Your course should always focus on one main niche, so you're able to create content that is in-demand, relevant, and focused.

At the same time, you don't want to box yourself into a corner. The topic you choose should be something you can see yourself still interested in a year from now.

You don't want the problem to be easily solvable, either. Your goal is to find a way to create a course that provides a workable system that addresses the issues people are struggling with.

By purchasing access to your course, they are given the knowledge needed to accomplish specific goals.

Most of the top-selling courses focus on one main subject. They expand their program by allowing students to either purchase additional access to upgrades or by offering additional resources after someone has graduated from the course.

Don't let anything stand in your way! Even if you aren't an expert on the topic, chances are you still have something worthy of teaching and that people will pay money for.

Keep in mind that you need to develop a strong hook for your membership program to be successful.

A hook reels you in. It sets your program apart. It works to differentiate your program from your competitors and tell potential subscribers why they benefit from signing up for your program. It's visceral and compelling.

Evaluate your membership program's strengths and unique benefits.

- How does it stand out?
- What is the greatest asset you offer members?
- How is it different?
- What will someone learn or improve by being a part of it?

Your task of the day

Step 1: Identify an ongoing problem in your niche where people seek guidance, training, and, ultimately, a solution.

Step 2: Create a list of topics that you should cover in your course based on those common questions. Then, decide on the various formats you plan to use (video, printables, workbooks, etc.)

Step 3: Next, go through that list and narrow your focus to target a specific segment of your market. Need help identifying a problem in your niche or coming up with a topic for your course?

Here are a few ways to uncover possibilities:

Send an email out to your mailing list that asks what your readers need help with. You can either set the email so they reply with their own feedback or choose 3-4 topics and create a survey that asks them to choose only one.

Discover ideas for your course by searching popular blogs and Facebook groups in your niche. See what people are talking about and what questions are commonly asked.

Search Reddit sub-threads as well as Q&A sites like Quora for popular questions and ongoing discussions. You want your course to be based on an evergreen, a common problem in your market.

Search platforms like Udemy.com and Teachable.com to see what courses are selling and what kind of training is being offered.

Sites like Teachable will show you a breakdown of all lesson plans so you can get a feel for the scope of the training and identify what could be missing. Then, include coverage in your own course to stand out in your market.

Tip: Creating a training program is easy with sites like https://www.Teachable.com because you aren't required to build your own website or learn HTML.

All you have to do is enter in your content or link to your videos, and Teachable will compile your course so that people can move through it at their own pace while keeping track of their progress.

Step-by-Step Brand Building Checklist

Here is my personal brand building checklist. I use this every time I launch a new business.

Setting the Tone

Okay, so this is the fun part of brand building. This is where you get to define your brand's visual image (look & feel), which includes:

- **Color Scheme**: What do you envision as the look and feel of your brand? What colors do you feel stand out? What kind of graphics do you plan to feature?

- **Graphics:** Depending on the type of business you are planning to launch, you'll want to consider hiring a professional graphic designer to create digital product images, banners, a logo, and other graphic elements that anchor your brand. You can hire people from places like www.Fiverr.com, or you can look for graphic designers from freelance markets like www.Upwork.com.

- **Domain & Website:** Register a domain that defines your brand in some way and set up a simple website using content management services like www.Wordpress.com. You can register a domain at www.NameCheap.com or www.GoDaddy.com for less than $12 a year and set up a hosting account with www.BlueHost.com or www.HostGator.com.

- **Social Accounts:** You'll want to quickly snag any social media accounts that you plan to use so that you can stake claim to your brand's username. This could be your website domain or perhaps a keyword-based name that attracts attention.
- **Track Your Customers & Traffic:** Integrate a site analytics tool into your website so that you can keep a steady pulse on where your traffic is coming from. This will help you later develop marketing campaigns that are geared towards your prime sources of traffic.

Resource: How to install Google Analytics: http://www.wpbeginner.com/beginnersguide/how-to-installgoogle-analytics-in-wordpress/

Applying Differentiators

Next, you'll want to look for ways you can stand apart from other than the visual look and feel of your brand's image. Here are a few ways to do that:

- **Create a Unique Tagline**
  A slogan is an important part of every brand because it simplifies your brand message and breaks it down into a few descriptive words.

A tagline is important because it helps to create an immediate connection between you and your customer. You're essentially acknowledging your audience's expectations and reinforcing your commitment to providing value.

As business owners in highly competitive markets, it's important to always go the extra mile in becoming memorable. A tagline can give you the instant recognition in crowded markets.

Not sure how to create an unforgettable tagline that helps to establish your brand?

Think of the following when coming up with your tagline:

- What impression do you want to make?
- What image do you want to convey?
- What words would you want them to use to describe your brand?

The bottom line is, the more specific, unique, and direct your brand is, the easier it will be to connect with your target audience, build a relationship with your customers based on trust and reliability, and, ultimately, sell more products.

When a potential customer purchases one of your products, you want them to know what to expect without having to think twice.

- **Connect Brand Elements**
  It's important always to connect every component of your business together to provide potential customers with different ways to reach out to you and become part of your tribe.

For example, you should always feature your social media links on your website so that people can follow you and begin to interact with you through multiple channels. The more often people see your social media links, the more likely they'll be to follow you.

There are plenty of free plugins to help you get the job done, including https://wordpress.org/plugins/shared-counts/ and https://wordpress.org/plugins/sassy-social-share/.

- **Provide Social Proof (if available):**
  People want to be reassured that you know what you're talking about and that your products have helped others in similar situations.

So, whenever possible, include testimonials and feedback from customers who have benefited from your products or services.

Positive reviews can be the driving force behind successful product launches, so don't overlook this!

Successful branding examples and how you can harness them

As we have seen throughout this book, there are many different ways that personal branding can be achieved. Yet they all start with the same foundation. Some brands are more successful than others.

Strong personal brands can be valuable, increasing exposure for any companies or ventures an individual decides to undertake. It is an excellent foundation for any future products or services.

Think about how many people with strong personal brands have written self-help books with their top tips for success — with their audiences fawning over the content and swearing by the tips to try and change their lives.

Emulating others' success can be a great way to bolster your personal branding; just make sure you are not copying it exactly.

Think about your favorite people and the personal branding they have curated. What associations do you have with them? Chances are there are a few keywords that spring to mind when you think of them. Now think about why those brands have those associations and what words you want people to think of when they think of you; because, with an effective branding strategy, they will think of you—just safeguard that it is in the way you want. These key traits are the cornerstone

Some of the most successful brands are also controversial. They are not afraid to alienate a considerable portion of the population to reach their desired audience. This has been essential to their relevance and achievements.

While, at times, these examples are controversial and do not appeal to everyone, by seeing the success of others, it can be easy to recognize areas of your own.

Steve Jobs

Even before he was Apple's face, he had a strong brand that he brought to the company. His personal branding was unique and strong—he understood what he wanted to convey, and his actions furthered this. There was a complete synergy between his purpose, message, and audience, which made him seem trustworthy and authentic.

Steve Jobs personified the ideas of innovation and created the next best thing he went on to do numerous times through the products he helped create. The purpose of his personal branding was clear, and he effectively communicated the messages he wanted to portray.

Steve Jobs created one of the most credible and recognizable brands, so much so that his legacy lives on and his branding messages and tips still remain relevant.

The Kardashian Family

The Kardashian Family is one of the best examples of successful branding. They were able to build an entire media empire and use their show to help control the narrative surrounding them. Even when faced with harsh media scandals, the Kardashians would share the raw and real insights into their personal lives, making their fans feel empathetic towards the sisters. Their personal branding makes you feel like you know them, given how much of their lives they exploit on their show and on their personal social media accounts.

Between them, they have released numerous products — from perfume to skincare to clothing lines. But the question is, would any of those products have been anywhere near as successful as they were if the Kardashian named had not been attached?

The Kardashians, love them, or hate them, have turned their name into such a successful brand that they could probably sell anything.

Hugh Hefner

A controversial figure, for sure, but can you seriously picture a silk robe without thinking about him?

While contentious, Hefner's personal branding and his company matched the lifestyle that he lived. This is a key aspect of his success. Had he headed up a conservative company, it would be confusing to reconcile that with his lifestyle choice.

Hugh Hefner is an excellent example of entwining your personal branding with your business and having a wider success level.

Now, think about your favorite brands

What is it about them that enchants you? How have they captured your attention? What springs to mind when you think about them? How do they use content? What makes them successful? What could they improve on?

Analyzing other brands, particularly ones in the same industry as you, will help you better define your personal branding strategy. You can exploit their missed opportunities, capitalize on their mistakes, and try to emulate their successes.

Conclusion

In conclusion, personal branding is essential to the success of any venture in the twenty-first century. While defining and outlining your personal branding can seem like a massive task at the outset, the rewards will be unparalleled. Doing so at the beginning of your entrepreneurial journey will give you a head start on your competition.

Creating a unique brand that stands out in your market and communicating to customers that you have something valuable to offer isn't as difficult as you may have thought.

The key is to define how your brand is different from others and why customers should choose you over the competition.

You do this by applying differentiators throughout your brand message and by creating a look and feel that speaks to your audience. Then, set the wheels in motion by connecting that brand message to products and services that offer clear value and go the extra mile.

Having a personal branding strategy will get you noticed; it will add authority to your content, encouraging your audience to engage with you.

This eBook has given you the strongest possible foundation to begin planning your personal branding strategy or updating and rejuvenating your current brand. While it can seem overwhelming, working through it methodically and ensuring you outline each section precisely will guarantee that you create the best brand possible before moving onto the next. Defining your audience, purpose, and message is a key branding strategy.

Building a strong foundation for your brand's concept will allow you to create meaningful content that will impact your audience. Your specific target audience will come to you once your content is out there waiting for them. Monitoring your analytics, and consequently, your influence is the best way to make sure that your branding is on track.

There is nothing wrong with trying something new; it is a fantastic opportunity to stand out. Make sure that you are keeping up with trends. This is both an industry but also medium-specific. Staying up to date with the kinds of content your audience wants to consume will ensure that your engagement stays high. Staying alert means that you can adapt and improve as necessary. Do not let the fear of trying something new or different stop you from trying to stand out. Businesses fail, but good brands last forever.

Real personal branding power is being able to influence the trends, not just keeping up with them.

Personal branding is the make or break of the business world; good branding means that you will have a strong connection with your audience—without that, you will not be successful.

Do not be afraid to shake things up! Your personal branding is what will allow you to live out your dreams fully. No one has ever made a difference in the world by following the rules.

CHECKLIST

- What can be incorporated into your personal branding?
    - Education
    - Passions
    - Goals
    - Past successes
    - Experience
    - Personality traits
    - Values
    - Beliefs
    - Interests
    - What motivates you?
    - What do you want to achieve?
- Who is your target audience demographic?
    - Age
    - Location
    - Gender
    - Lifestyle
    - Education
    - Financial situation
    - Technological use
    - Family/living situation
- How can you understand your target audience better psychologically?
    - What do they want?
    - What do they need?
    - What challenges do they face?
    - What do they believe in?
    - What are their attitudes and behaviors?
- What does your personal branding have to offer?
    - Are you making their life easier or solving a problem?
    - Are you making their life more entertaining?

- o Are you helping them?
- o Are you teaching them something?
- o Why should they care?

- The three keys to success
  - o Audience
    - Do not try and appeal to everyone
      - Clearly defining who your audience is
    - Understanding your target audience
    - Knowing what they want
    - Sharing their values
    - Catering your content towards them
    - Sharing it in places where they will find it
  - o Authenticity
    - Seeming "real"
    - Sharing your story
    - Being accountable
    - Make them trust you
  - o Consistency
    - Posting content consistently
    - Good quality content
    - Quality is more important than quantity
    - Design consistency
      - Logo
      - Font
      - Headshots
      - Design colors
    - Audience engagement
      - Are they liking your posts?
      - Commenting?
      - Sharing?
      - Or ignoring?
    - Replying to messages or comments

- What social media are you using?
  - Claim usernames
  - Make profiles
    - Website
    - Facebook
    - Twitter
    - Instagram
    - Pinterest
    - Blog
    - LinkedIn
    - Email
    - YouTube
    - Podcasts
  - Be active
  - Use the ones that your target audience does
  - Have contact pages
  - Share posts between platforms to increase traffic
  - Have a call to action
- Strategies to grow your brand and audience
  - Original content creation
    - Images and photoshoots
    - Videos
    - Podcasts
    - Blogs
  - Mailing list
    - Newsletter
    - Link back to posts
    - Exclusive content
    - Previews
    - Build subscribers
  - Free content as a preview
  - Networking
    - Guest blogs
    - Features or profiles
    - Interviews

- Conferences
- Exposure to new audiences
- Get discovered by other reputable brands
- Collaborations
  - Offering incentives
  - Direct, personal communication
- Building a connection with your audience
  - Responding promptly and personally
  - Replying to comments or questions
  - Taking on feedback
  - In-person events
  - Live sessions online
  - Starting a Facebook group to interact with your audience
- Are you checking your analytics to track your branding progress?
  - Engagement levels
    - Likes
    - Comments
    - Shares
  - Compared with views
  - Insights into post reach
  - Click-through rate
  - Are your followers translating into success stories?
  - Are you reaching your target audience?
  - Is your posting schedule appropriate?
  - Search engine optimisation
    - Can you be found?
    - Keywords and phrases
  - Public image
- Ways to use your personal branding in your everyday life
  - Not just about a digital footprint
  - Business cards
  - Dress well

- o Network
- o Be authentic
- o Sharing your story
- Other things to think about when creating your personal brand
  - o What words do you want to come to mind when your audience thinks of your brand?
  - o How do you want to be perceived?
  - o Famous brands in your industry?
    - How to stand out from them?
  - o Successful brands that you like?
    - Why do you like them?
    - How can you copy parts of their success?
    - How can you improve on them?
  - o Successful brands that you do not like?
    - Why not?
    - How can you improve?
  - o What kind of content will best share you message?
  - o Will your current actions help you build your dream life and create your personal branding?

www.ingramcontent.com/pod-product-compliance
Lightning Source LLC
Chambersburg PA
CBHW070406220526
45467CB00001B/491